THIS BOOK BELONGS TO

_____

God Loves Me! Coloring and Activity Book for Kids by Melanie Salas
Published by Golden Crown Publishing, LLC

www.GoldenCrownPublishing.com

Created by Melanie Salas

ISBN: 978-1-954648-21-0

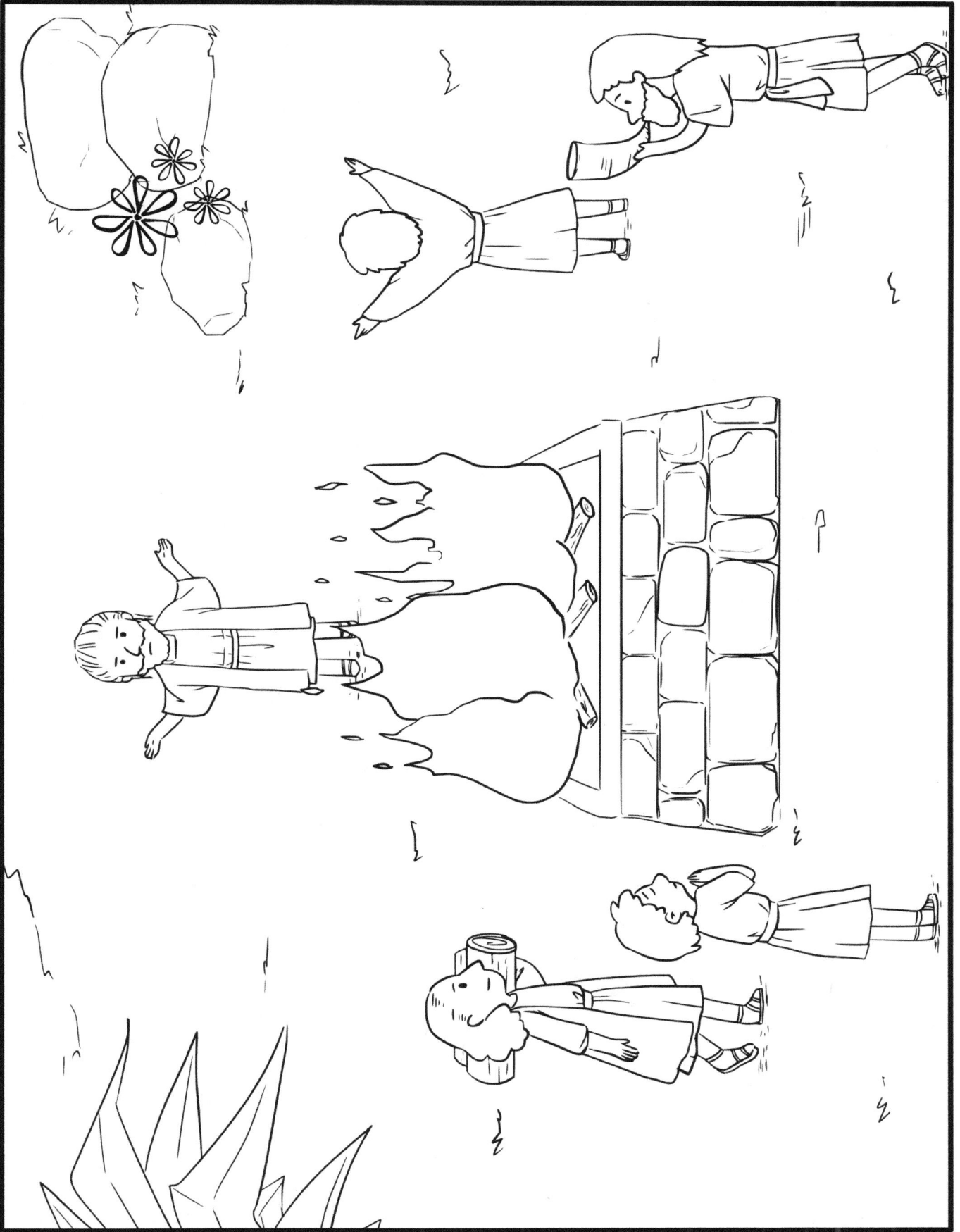

www.ingramcontent.com/pod-product-compliance
Lightning Source LLC
Chambersburg PA
CBHW081240020426

42331CB00013B/3233